A CHRISTMAS WORSHIP EXPERIENCE

CREATED BY
REGI STONE & J. DANIEL SMITH

ARRANGED & ORCHESTRATED BY
J. DANIEL SMITH

NARRATIONS BY MIKE HARLAND

PRODUCTS AVAILABLE

Listening CDs are available at a reduced rate when purchased in quantities of 10 or more.

WORSHIP MUSIC GROUP

1-4158-5584-6

FOREWORDS

Christmas is my favorite time of year. This most special season is when we celebrate the birth of Jesus and enjoy making memories with our family and friends. Can you imagine a world without Christmas? I certainly can't. Our world wouldn't be the same without Christmas because we would be without Christ. We attempted to choose songs for this musical that would create an opportunity for your choir, worship team, and congregation to experience Christmas like never before. One of the highlights for me was working with LifeWay and J. Daniel Smith. All who have had the honor of singing Dan's arrangements know what a gift he is to all of us. I applaud LifeWay for their commitment to publish quality music with a message. It is my prayer that this collection will spark a wonderful moment of passionate worship within your church family as you lift your voices to sing.

Merry Christmas!

Regi Stone

Don't most things you really want to communicate effectively start with the phrase "You know"? It's as if we are prefacing our comment by saying, "I really need you to hear what I'm saying because it's coming from my heart, and I truly mean it." I suppose I'll just have to start my message to you in that way.

You know, it has been an amazing, incredible experience to be the arranger and orchestrator of such a terrific musical. From the very first developmental meeting to the final touches of the mix, every phase of it has been nothing short of delightful. Mike Harland's wonderfully composed narrations and gentle guidance, along with the artistry that Bruce Cokeroft brings in concept development and his unique instinct for knowing just the right songs to assemble, make for the best possible start in creating a work such as this. Then add the Spirit-led worship leading style and vocal ability of Regi Stone, and you have nothing short of a winner! By the way, when I get to heaven, I hope to sing just like Regi…surely the Lord will allow that. In case I have not made it clear, I'm quite a fan of these gentlemen, and I am grateful for the ease they brought to this process. What you will find here is not just great songs woven together, though that would be enough, given the strength of these tunes. Within these pages, you are going to find the opportunity to once again tell the story you've been telling for years, but in a fresh, contempo-rary way. I know it's becoming an almost worn-out phrase, but let me say clearly that this is a worship experience for Christmas. I'll go a step further. When you listen to the entire musical, I promise you'll be touched by the truth of the message and the power of the music as you simply take another look at the Christ of Christmas.

Blessings to you for this holiday season,

J. Daniel Smith

PUBLISHER'S NOTE

Whether you use *Imagine* in its entirety as a worship service, or simply as a seasonal worship song resource, you will find it to be a relevant collection of music for your church. It also offers a wonderful collection of current praise and worship songs by leading writers/artists such as Chris Tomlin, David Crowder, and Matt Redman, combined with newly written worship songs and familiar carols. The options for vocal praise teams and soloists, along with flexible narrations, will provide your ministry with an array of performance possibilities.

Consider using the Accompaniment DVD. It contains quality corresponding video segments and selected corporate worship moments, including song lyrics, for certain songs. Also included are two performance options: a split track accompaniment mix, which contains the performance track on one channel and the choral vocals (minus solos) on the other, and a click track mix for those who wish to use the DVD with live orchestra. With this option, count-offs precede each song segment with a click track on one channel throughout, and choral vocals (minus solos) on the other as a reference. Of course, the usual companion products are available, such as posters, bulletins, and studio orchestrations.

May God richly bless you in the presentation of *Imagine—A Christmas Worship Experience*.

LifeWay Worship

INSTRUMENTATION

INSTRUMENTATION: Flute 1-2, Oboe, Clarinet 1-2, Alto Sax, Tenor Sax, Trumpet 1, Trumpet 2-3, Horn 1-2, Trombone 1-2, Trombone 3/(opt. Tuba), Percussion 1-2, Harp, Rhythm, Violin 1-2, Viola, Cello, String Bass.

SUBSTITUTE PARTS: Alto Sax 1-2 (substitute for French Horn), Tenor Sax/Baritone Treble Clef (substitute for Trombone 1-2), Clarinet 3 (substitute for Viola), Bass Clarinet (substitute for Cello), Keyboard String Reduction.

The rhythm part in this orchestration is designed to provide satisfying accompaniment throughout. However, keyboard players may find it helpful to reference certain passages in the choral score to supply the most supportive accompaniment.

PRODUCTION TEAM
Craig Adams, Ronnie Clark, Bruce Cokeroft, Deborah Hickerson, Sarah Huffman, Chad Hunter, Wendell McGuirk, Lee Ann Roberts, Keith Wilbanks, and Danny Zaloudik.

TABLE OF CONTENTS

Imagine a World Without Christmas
(Opening)

Words and Music by
REGI STONE and JEFF FERGUSON
Arranged by J. Daniel Smith

29

men from a - far___ that had fol - lowed the star___ did not come.___

Gm²   F²/A

31

rit.   *p*

Im -

E♭²   E♭   Gm/A   A⁷♭9

rit.

33 *a tempo*

ag - ine a world with - out___ Je - sus;___ just

D   DM⁷   D   G²   G   A/G   G

p a tempo

35 *mp*

tell me, where would___ we all be?___ No

D   DM⁷   G⁶9

Son of God born,____ and be - liev - ers no more___ would be -

lieve.

Narrator: "Imagine a world . . ."

Underscore

"History tells us . . ."

Faster ♩ = **115**

Segue to "O Praise Him"

NARRATION 1

NARRATOR 1: Imagine a world without Jesus. For many of us, that would be difficult to do. But there was a time when all the world knew was a world without Christ—a time when there was no Messiah, no joy, and no peace. History tells us that for 400 years preceding the birth of Jesus, there was no record that God had spoken to His people. For *400 years*, all they had known was the rule of foreign kings, the oppression of evil empires, and a God they could not hear. Where was Jehovah? Where was the promised Messiah?

(music begins to "O Praise Him [All This for a King]")

Then, when the moment would finally come for God to speak, the silence would be shattered by the cry of a newborn child! Jesus, the Living Word, would become flesh and dwell among them. Imagine the joy, imagine the worship, imagine the glory of His praise!

O Praise Him (All This for a King)

with

O Come, All Ye Faithful

Words and Music by
DAVID CROWDER
Arranged by J. Daniel Smith

† "O Come, All Ye Faithful." Words: Latin hymn; ascribed to JOHN FRANCIS WADE; tr. FREDERICK OAKELEY, and others. Music: JOHN FRANCIS WADE.

NARRATION 2

NARRATOR 1: Lord, You *are* holy! You *are* the Living Word of God! We praise You! We adore You! *(music begins to "Made to Worship")* You are the Light that came to the darkness; the Creator that came so all creation could worship You. O Lord, fill our hearts tonight. Let us worship You now!

(As an option, Narration 2 may be delivered by the worship leader.)

Made to Worship

Words and Music by
CHRIS TOMLIN, ED CASH,
and STEPHAN SHARP
Arranged by J. Daniel Smith

(Soloist continues with Men, 1st time;
may ad lib, 2nd time)
CHOIR *mf*

He has filled our hearts with won - der___

so that we al - ways re - mem - ber:___

Soloist ad lib around Choir
you and I___ are made___ to wor - ship, you and I___ are called___ to love,___

SOLO with some freedom

All we are,___ and all we have,___ is

all a gift___ from God___ that we___ re - ceive._____

CODA

original lyric "who"

you___ and I will see___ *that we___ were meant_ to be.___

CODA

And e - ven the rocks___ cry out,___ and e - ven the heav - ens shout_

at the___ sound of His ho - ly___ name._____

So let ev-'ry voice_ sing out,_ and let ev-'ry knee_ bow down._

_ He is wor - thy of all_ our praise._

SOLO

You and I_ are made_ to wor - ship, you and I_ are called_ to love,_

sub. *mp*

original lyric "who"

you___ and I will see___ *that we___ were meant___ to be,___

*that we___ were meant___ to be,___

we were meant___ to be,___

Soloist may offer up words of praise to God over final held chord.

NARRATION 3

(music begins to "Glory in the Highest")

NARRATOR 2: It began with just one angel at first—"Glory to God in the highest, and on earth peace" to all men *(Luke 2:14, KJV)*. But how could just one angel be enough for this unbelievable announcement? You can almost imagine as the angel chorus slowly builds to proclaim: "Glory to God! Glory to God!"

Glory in the Highest

with

Angels We Have Heard on High

Words and Music by
CHRIS TOMLIN, DANIEL CARSON, ED CASH,
JESSE REEVES, and MATT REDMAN
Arranged by J. Daniel Smith

Narrator: "It began with . . ."

"But how could just one . . ."

You are the first. You go be-fore. You are the last.

† "Angels We Have Heard on High"

† "Angels We Have Heard on High." Words and Music: Traditional French Carol.

42

PRAISE TEAM

Glo - - - - -

(CHOIR)

__ high - est.__ Glo - ry in the __ high - est.__

A   D² 　 A

ri - a.

__ Glo - ry in the __ high - est.__ to You, __ Lord,

D²   A   D²

(music begins to "Cry in the Dark")

NARRATOR 1: Just imagine young Mary on her way to the manger. This ordinary girl, chosen by God to bear His Son—now moments away from giving birth—and Joseph, a simple carpenter about to become the earthly father of the Maker and Lord over all the earth. The moments grew tense as the time drew near—and then, at the precise moment ordained before time began, a baby's cry pierced the silence of the world—a little baby, destined to be the Savior of mankind.

Cry in the Dark

Words and Music by
REGI STONE and
CHRISTY SUTHERLAND DUDNEY
Arranged by J. Daniel Smith

† "O Little Town of Bethlehem." Music: LEWIS H. REDNER.

beau-ti-ful start,___ with one ba-by's cry___ in the dark.___

All the earth stood

All the earth stood_ still___

still_____ at His voice. Ah_____

at the sound of His voice.___

Ev - 'ry beat of His heart____ ech - oed my name.____

God's per - fect plan____ was born in a man.____ What a

beau - ti - ful start,____ with one ba - by's cry____ in the dark,____

NARRATION 5

(music begins to "Only the Son of God")

NARRATOR 1: So it was for us that He came that night so long ago in Bethlehem. But this was only the beginning of His relentless, loving pursuit of our hearts. Christ Jesus, who being in very nature, God, did not consider equality with God something to be grasped, but made Himself nothing, taking the very nature of a servant, being made in human likeness, and being found in appearance as a man, He humbled Himself and became obedient to death—even death on a cross *(Phil. 2:5-8).*

Only the Son of God

Words and Music by
REGI STONE and
DAVID M. EDWARDS
Arranged by J. Daniel Smith

Soloist continues with Sop. (ad lib)

Glo - ry__ to__ on - ly__ You;__

Je - sus, the Son__ of__ God._____ All

prais - es__ to__ on - ly__ You;__

that Je-sus would come_____ to make__ us free?__

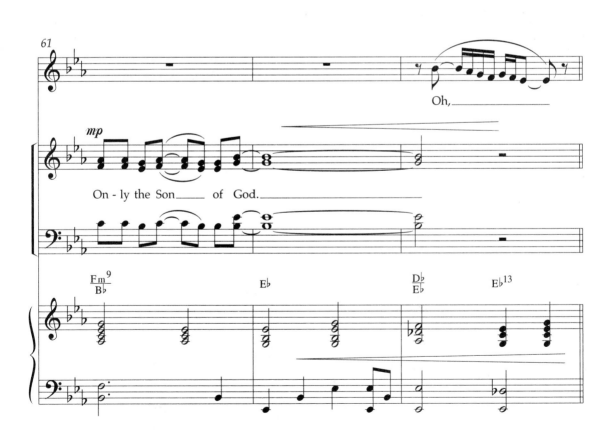

Oh,_____

On - ly the Son_____ of God._____

NARRATION 6

(music begins to "Joy!")

NARRATOR 1: The prophet Isaiah described, in part, who the Son of God would be. He would be a Wonderful Counselor, the Mighty God, the Everlasting Father, and the Prince of Peace. Isaiah 9:2 tells us that, "The people walking in darkness have seen a great light." Many years later, the Apostle John said Jesus was that Light, now shining in a world of darkness.

(music begins to change)

NARRATOR 2: Imagine all that Jesus brought to the world when He came that first Christmas night: hope...love...grace, and forgiveness! The familiar Christmas carol proclaims "Light and life to all He brings!"[1] Jesus Christ, the Light of the world, brought power and strength, life and freedom! He was born to bring us a reason to live and a way to know God. He has brought all this and more! Our Savior has come to bring us joy!

[1]From "Hark! The Herald Angels Sing," words by Charles Wesley, alt. by George Whitfield.

Joy!

Words by
REGI STONE and
GERON DAVIS

Music by
GERON DAVIS
Arranged by J. Daniel Smith

"The familiar Christmas carol proclaims . . ."

(drum fill)

NARRATION 7

NARRATOR 2: With all that Jesus brought into our lives, *(music begins to "Jesus, Light of the World")* what can we bring Him in return? Some of the first visitors to see the Baby were wise men from the east. They brought gifts of great worth—gold, frankincense, and myrrh. Imagine the thrill they must have felt as they approached the young family with such extravagant offerings.

We can do no less. We come to worship our King—the One who shines His light into our lives. And just like those men of so long ago, we now offer *our* most precious possession—our very own hearts and lives.

Jesus, Light of the World

Words and Music by
BRAD AVERY, DAVID CARR, MAC POWELL,
MARK LEE, and TAI ANDERSON
Arranged by J. Daniel Smith

94

NARRATION 8

(music begins to "Glorious")

NARRATOR 1: Whenever we're in the presence of greatness, words often fail us. Imagine the words that came to mind when those that gathered around the manger first saw Jesus. How could they have found a way to express their wonder and worship in the presence of the promised One? Did they simply bow in silence as they worshiped Him?

Tonight we gather to bow before this same King. He is all they hoped He would be—Ruler of all—One whose kingdom would never end.

He is wonderful!...Jesus is glorious!

Glorious

Words and Music by
CHRIS TOMLIN
and JESSE REEVES
Arranged by J. Daniel Smith

ri - ous. There is a King that we a -

dore. With hum-ble hearts we bow be - fore You,

Lord. There is a place we long to

61

47

WORSHIP LEADER *f*

Maj - es -

(CHOIR)

ri - ous.

C   C²(no3)   Am   Am/G

64

ty   and pow - er___   are Yours_ a - lone_ for - ev - er.___

f

Ah___

F   Am   Am/G   F²   F

(music begins)

NARRATOR/WORSHIP LEADER: Holy is Your name, Lord. You are worthy of all praise.
So we lift our voices and sing, "Hallelujah to You."

Hallelujah to You

Words and Music by
REGI STONE and
DAVID M. EDWARDS
Arranged by J. Daniel Smith

NARRATION 10

(This narration may also be delivered by the pastor or worship leader.)

(music begins to "Imagine a World Without Christmas")

NARRATOR 1/PASTOR/WORSHIP LEADER: In Frank Capra's Christmas classic, *It's a Wonderful Life*, the main character, George Bailey, is given a rare opportunity—the chance to see what the world would have been like if he had never been born. He learns quickly that his life affected many people, and that the world would have been a very different place without him. Imagine the same question about Jesus. What if? What if Jesus had never been born?

What about you? If you have never received God's gift of love through Jesus, then, for you, it's almost as if He has not been born at all. He may have come to save the world, but has Jesus come into *your* life?

You don't have to leave this place wondering what it's like to know this Savior! Jesus is real! And He is ready to come into your world, cleanse your heart with His grace, and fill you with His peace. You can ask Him to come into your life…right now.

(If desired, an extended time of invitation or call to commitment may be given prior to the next song.)

Imagine a World Without Christmas
(Full version)

Words and Music by
REGI STONE and
JEFF FERGUSON
Arranged by J. Daniel Smith

† "Glory in the Highest"

Narrator: "In Frank Capra's Christmas classic, . . ."

"Imagine the same question . . ."

"You don't have to leave . . ."

† *"Imagine a World Without Christmas"*

SOLO (WORSHIP LEADER)

Im-

ag - ine a world__ with - out__ Christ - mas; a

place with-out hol - i - day____ cheer,____ where we'd nev - er find____ the most____ won - der - ful time____ of____ the____ year.____ Im - ag - ine a world____ with - out____ Je - sus;____ just

126

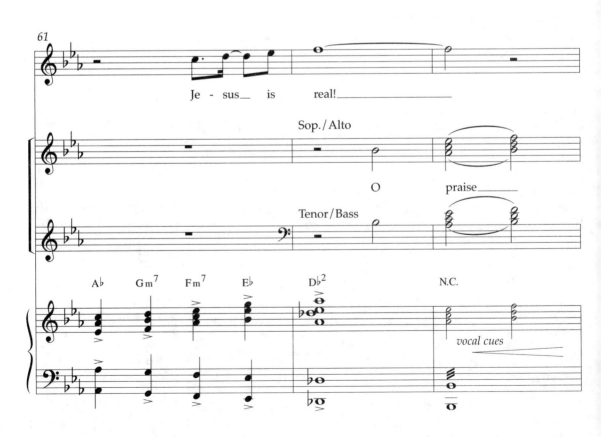

NARRATION 11

(music begins to "Finale")

NARRATOR 1: Tonight we don't have to imagine the world without Jesus. He *is* Emmanuel, God with us, and nothing can separate us from His love.

Now we can do what the shepherds and wise men did—we can live a life of praise and obedience to show our love for the One who gave His life for us. It's what we're created to do. We can—we must worship Jesus!

Finale

includes

If You Know You're Loved, Made to Worship, *and* Glory in the Highest

with Angels We Have Heard on High

Arranged by J. Daniel Smith

If you know you're loved_ by the King,_ live_ for Him, live_ for Him!_

If you know you're loved_ by the King,_ live_ for Him, live_ for Him!

If you know you're loved_ by the King,_ then sing,_ sing,_ sing!_____

If you know you're loved_ by the King,_ sing,_ sing,_ sing!_

Then live_ for Him,_ live_ for Him._

If you know you're loved_ by the King,_ live_ for Him, live_ for Him!

If you know you're loved_ by the King,_ sing,_ sing,_ sing!_____

If you know you're loved_ by the King,_ sing,_ sing,_ sing!_

31
If you know you're loved _ by the King, _ then live _ for Him, _ live _ for Him! _____

If you know you're loved _ by the King, _ live _ for Him, live _ for Him! _____

D⁷/A   G²

57

33
____   Oh, _____

D   D/C♯

you and I____ are for-giv-en and free.____ (When)

You and I____ em-brace_ sur-ren - der, (when) you and I____choose to____be-lieve,_ (then)

* original lyric "who"

you____ and I will see____ *that we___were meant_ to be,___

Tempo I ♩ = 74

† "Glory in the Highest" *with* †† "Angels We Have Heard on High"

PRAISE TEAM

Glo - - - - high - est.__ Glo - ry in the__ high - est.__

ri - a. Glo - ry in the__ high - est,__ to You,__ Lord,__

B♭   E♭²   B♭

E♭²   B♭   E♭²

to You, Lord, to You, Lord,

to You, Lord,

to You, Lord!

to You, Lord!